WE WHO ARE NOT DEAD YET

poems

Aryan Kaganof

Mwanaka Media and Publishing Pvt Ltd,
Chitungwiza Zimbabwe

*

Creativity, Wisdom and Beauty

Publisher: *Mmap*
Mwanaka Media and Publishing Pvt Ltd
24 Svosve Road, Zengeza 1
Chitungwiza Zimbabwe
mwanaka@yahoo.com
mwanaka13@gmail.com
www.africanbookscollective.com/publishers/mwanaka-media-and-publishing
https://facebook.com/MwanakaMediaAndPublishing/

Distributed in and outside N. America by African Books Collective
orders@africanbookscollective.com
www.africanbookscollective.com

ISBN: 978-1-77928-535-5
EAN: 9781779285355

© Aryan Kaganof 2025

All rights reserved.
No part of this book may be reproduced or transmitted in any form or by any means, mechanical or electronic, including photocopying and recording, or be stored in any information storage or retrieval system, without written permission from the publisher

DISCLAIMER
All views expressed in this publication are those of the author and do not necessarily reflect the views of *Mmap*.

Contents

Introduction	04
Movement 1	05
Shadows and Treasons (a cento for Mphutlane wa Bofelo)	06
Cento for David wa Maahlamela	08
Cento with Whiskey and Eliot	16
Born Again (A Cento for Eugene Skeef)	17
Cento for Nicola Deane	21
Cento for Lesego Rampolokeng	22
Cento for Carina Venter	23
Cento #113 Molloy, blinded (for Samuel Beckett)	24
We Who Are Not Dead Yet	25
Movement II	29
How I Passed For White	30
Theophany	32
Stellenbosched	34
Palimpsestina 4.33	37
Palimpsestina 4.33a	38
Palimpsestina 4.33b	39
Movement III	
The Palimpsestina	42
Movement IV	85
Stellenbosched Again	86
The Disappearance of the Actress (Cento for Two)	93

Introduction

My Publisher, Tendai Rinos Mwanaka, asked me to write an Introduction but I did not want to write an Introduction because I was tired of all those poets and their Introductions, so why become one of them? So instead I cut and pasted what Tendai had written on Facebook earlier the same day (Thursday 18 September, 2025), yes this is what he wrote: "Once in a while I get a manuscript, book that really challenges, confounds or makes me feel like I am reading my own poetry... WE WHO ARE NOT DEAD YET by Aryan Kaganof—which I was editing—does all those three things to me. Aryan is my twin, he writes visual filmic poetry that doesn't care about rules of writing, poetry making etc... you feel like you are watching a crazy monologue film of a character bent on shitting on you." So that's the Introduction and, no, I'm not shitting you.

Aryan Kaganof
Thursday 18 September 2025

Movement I

"By stretching language we'll distort it sufficiently
to wrap ourselves in it and hide."
                                    Jean Genet.

Shadows and Treasons (a cento for Mphutlane wa Bofelo)

On Thursday 16 August
the sheriff came but the poet
was on leave so instead of fur
niture the poems were attached
they left the
books unopened
so they did not find
the ransom note and
the trickledown economics

        never
        trickled

On Thursday 16 August
the wind conspired to carry his
sad poems away beyond the boom
gates that separated his grassroots stompies
from his born again cigar chompers

        flashback

the poet before
he committed treason
was exhorting his people
to wake up "you are the children
of slaves" (what they did not expect
was they they would become the parents
of slaves too)

        fast for
        ward

to the end of treason villification
of dissent breeds parrots, either

you are with god or you are a
soft target. then the poet
had to kill his own
poems or
face exe
cution
what
would
you have
done? O worthy
people of Mzansi
what did he do? he chose
treason above money even though
he realised that only money has a voice
or should i say, his jitas chose treason for him
and so the people of Mzansi followed the sheriff's orders
and cut all his tongues out one by one, slowly, left him skinless

        freeze frame

with no poems to protect him from the inferno. there was
not even enough of him left over for an identity crisis.
he took it on good faith that his crime was treason.
the choice was very clear. the choice is always
clear in Mzansi. either you have a credit
card or you die
nothing in be
tween.

        blackout

the flames licked up
and charred his many
treasons. his blood boiled
his corpse stank to high heaven
we stood around and heaved a great

sigh of relief, without the poet's treasons
it was so much easier to swallow the lies we
had been fed instead of our promised freedoms
he only spoke to shadows anyway

                    shadows and
                    treasons

Cento for David wa Maahlamela

Dear David,

perhaps you were not yet born
when poetry ambushed you
and fed you poison only
to find cement
pavements
have no
lips

to carry

her pots of
crucified tears
cracked, and leave
them broken like omens
that speak without voices
of the only viscous
earthly love you

ever tasted

If only
you
had a
pair of
scissors to
be sprinkled
with holy water
undressing withered
leaves the hot-headed
word empress and no one

understands
there is nothing to negotiate

Dear David,

I'm here in your country
for only a week hoping

the sky will weep
for me and I
hate it
when
you
tell me
such truth

I dislike to hear,
truth warmer, I should
say, than death because you
never allowed it to happen again
the entire truth is eaten without porridge
or rice and no piano shall speak again nothing
is sweet about this sea

Dear David,

Like a Bible about to be read
with all big books it bled
one cold afternoon you
said love is a step
mother, they say
sculpt me a
new heart
make use
of the
things

around you
and yes, the
garbage truck
as if to say: people

are clothes, your clothes

You've worn many people in the
past, you say I had hoped that this
common thing would collect us perhaps
you'll then admit you said nothing about
yourself or your
sins.

Dear David,

It is not yet my turn,
I will die another day

the impossible day.
No need for ambi
valent thoughts
I do it on a
piece of
paper
with
nobody
and nothing

in my head so
i can speak
melodies
of
repentance

You

told me
it's too early.
I see your mole
fingers digging me
out of the grave. to you
i return in needles of winter
raindrops because i will take no
pen nor paper
when I go

Dear David,

You know the essence of wounds
My God is a tongue that speaks

with lips sealed and stitched.
(S)He knows (s)he will soon
be bread
to worms
those without
shadows are here

again. their words are
always dressed to kill in echoes.
People have ice memories in this world
of machines double pay
double
pay

Dear David,

I remain an ordinary poet and when
the night shadows fall I return
to my makeshift poems
I call home. I took it to the street
I became against war and we bleed each time

we smile
In this country,
it is not the smile
that matters, released
behind closed doors does
it even have a name? Is that
even important? You are a literate
someone. You live here.

Dear David,

Lucifer used to envy you, I heard
maybe, just maybe "From ashes to ashes…"
A diamond is forever –

they were told especially when they return
from their armpit lovers now
that his pockets are suffocated by silver
and gold, how skeletal is the line between
patriotism and arrogance and I walked it

Dear David,

it's a matter of life and debt, we collided
with the midnight
and we were satisfied
to stomp the soil
and clothe us with the red
blanket. I could count bones of what
used to be poetry. Dear David,
I want to come to you to
meet the tree that
fruited you with
dirges
perhaps
this is what

the poem means
perhaps there are
no rules and if you
were to be amputated
with heavy nonsense

even if you were
stillborn again
poetry, real
poetry,
will
still
walk barefoot
on ghetto paper,

contentedly, have you
discovered your
uncommon
gift yet?

Dear David,

How can death
intimidate you?
Everything is dressed
with dust even the white
linen poems you washed not
so long ago though your heart
was full of mopani worms.
do the dead know
any distance
when they
jive?

Dear David,

Your breath is a verse
There's a poem in your
skull Where the sun
cannot steal
the marrow
of your
bones

anymore.

Sincerely,

AK

Cento with Whiskey and Eliot

i'm invisible without whiskey
if you do not come too close
i'm invisible without whiskey

wrinkles and slides i am here
still invisible without whiskey
lifting heavy feet in clumsy shoes

i'm invisible without whiskey
it was not (to start again) what one had expected
i'm invisible without whiskey

you say i am repeating something i have said before
i'm invisible without whiskey
but the faith and the love and the hope are all in the waiting

i'm invisible without whiskey
here and there does not matter
i'm invisible without whiskey

isolated with no before and after
i'm invisible without whiskey
and found and lost again and again

i'm invisible without whiskey
if to be warmed, then i must freeze
i'm invisible without whiskey

Born Again (A Cento for Eugene Skeef)

i

The elephant and the mantis tiptoed
past my sleeping mother's bedroom window
and into the starlit night (She was dreaming
of the ghost I would become)
I felt the cool soil under my unborn feet
as I slowly started to move out of her tunnel
and take my place in the World of the Perplexed
so that by the time my head got out
I was squealing perfectly in time
to the Elephant's drum
and the jig of the Mantis
that welcomed me
out of the womb
into this place
of unhealed
silence:

There was a knock on the door.
        The Elephant opened the door.
              It was Time outside.
                      The Mantis said "Come on in."

Then Time came in and suddenly I understood
that I would have to die one day
in order to become the Holy
Ghost my mother had dreamed.
So the Elephant, the Mantis, Time and I
all went in search of a slaughterhouse.

The clearing had been denuded of buildings by the relentless bombing.
All you could hear was the whisper of the waves of the ocean of blood.

I stood with the Elephant on my left and the Mantis on my Right
while Time started softly dancing onstage,
moving from side to side to the minimalist
        double-beat
of the sacred
        bantwak drum.

Then our voices combined and rose
as we opened the Gates of our Silence
where the umbilical cord
of our nation's ghost
had been buried
        without being named.

And for the benefit of the Perplexed
there will be a delayed scream,
        'The explosion
    will not happen today   it is too soon."

ii

When the time came for the executioner to sing
you were sitting in a garishly lit pizzeria
nursing a slice of the blood Moon
slowly detaching yourself
from every possible consequence,
one by one, before they, inevitably,
        came back to haunt you.

First you had an emotion,
then you shared that emotion,
then that emotion got returned,
but, finally, after a lot of commotion,
the emotions all got burned.

Then eventually you understood that you were disappearing,
and with you, every trace of the world you'd previously inhabited.
Once ago you'd have re-written an epic
lyric Cento about this insight,
today it hardly seems worth re-tweeting.

And thank you for coming by
   To partake in my torture
   Thank you for salting the wound,
   Thank you for the wonderful Q&A
   That robbed me of my last secrets,
   I had no right to those secrets anyway
   Please don't forget to register
   For next week's Zoom Meeting
                then it's lights out as you take your final curtain
call.

So many hours wasted.
So many pots of gold gone, gone to rainbows.
And while all of this was going on,
you took your mask off,
and watched, and waited.

And all this patient waiting was incremental.
Increments of blood and stone.
        Increments of gristle and bone.
Increments of gristle and bone.
        Increments of blood and stone.
So many lonely hours wasted.

Then you stepped outside of your comfort zone,
stripped your accomplices to their bones.
What you saw under their skin
merely confirmed what you already knew:
so many hours wasted.

It was an hour to go before the last
Mask came with your robust executioner in it.
There was no time left to negotiate terms
they only spoke in cash.

You watched from the shadows
as first your reputation went up in flames
and when those flames calmed back to ash
it was time for your body to burn.

By now this final episode was being livestreamed
You changed your pronouns,
Held both your palms up to the blood Moon
    In the right palm was your Mantis,
    In the left your Elephant
You said goodby to Time again,
    to the World of the Perplexed.
                      Exeunt.
And were reborn,
débrouillard.

Cento for Nicola Deane

The archive must bleed
across the pulse
            therefore sound actually battles vision
interrogating the conclusion as a work of
return to touch

fragmented and/or destabilising

I see that I have never told you
how I listen to the vibrations
of my own tympanic membrane

An archive recycles endlessly
by composing the elements
of what one has experienced

                      into
                      traces
                      of blood
                                beating.

Cento for Lesego Rampolokeng

against my woken sensibilities
licking the boot that kicks it
in a ball-pointed moment
but who am i to talk?
slowing down when i   ebbed
hanging towards dignity
                      soil to soil
                              this is an ambush
                                            let's turn the history
page
    against my broken sensibilities
kicking the tongue that licks it
in a ball-punctured moment
but who am i to scream?
                the word is in me
formally sharpened
chopped up
sharpened
formally
word
me

Cento for Carina Venter

At the age of four I wanted to be a toyboy
at the age of three I wanted to be sixtysix feet tall
at the age of seven, a heartbreak player
at 24 I wanted to be the best-smelling book in the world
at 27 I wanted to be undead and buried.

    Now, on the subject of castration, let me say something else.
As one grows older, I find,
these words fold into
and inbetween one another,
not unlike your person and mine.

    A self cuts a self
I have dreamt, for example,
about stumbling over my own corpse.
Naked, my back turned to her,
face and torso visible through the flames.

    Her hands on my shoulders.
Gently, kneading, teaching me a lesson in openness; teaching me
how to unclench my peaches,
uncross my consonants, how to glissando.

There we sat, quietly, orderly, stoically.
So many things I wanted to be
At the age of three.

    What are these insignificant sad nostalgias
of mine anyway?   They mean nothing.

Cento #113 Molloy, blinded (for Samuel Beckett)

Let me hear nothing of the moon,
in my night there is no moon,
and if it happens that I speak of the stars
it is by mistake. To absence perhaps,
you must return, that's all I know,
it's misery to stay, misery to go.

There were times I forgot
not only who I was,
but that I was,
forgot to be.
Yes, the words I heard,
were heard as pure sounds,
free of all meaning,

and the words I uttered myself,
were often to me as the buzzing of an insect.
It seemed to me that all language
was an excess of language.

And what I saw was more like a crumbling,
a frenzied collapsing of all that protected me
from all I was condemned to be.
For I had no illusions,

I knew that all was about to end,
or to begin again,
it little mattered which,
and it little mattered how,
I had only to wait.
I closed my eyes.

We Who Are Not Dead Yet

I

I was in the shower reading Hegel
The water was scorching and the pages
became too hot to turn but, hey, that's OK
Hegel's not much of a page turner anyway.
Then I realized in a flash merely having a
shower to Be in was already privileged
despite anything Hegel had to say and
the abjection of all those bodies cla
m
ouring for running
water was literally built
into the structure of my hot
shower. Master Slave was in
herited through the pores of our
skin. I turned up the temperature
until that very un-melaninated
skin I was roasting in could
accurately be described
as post-Hegelian.

II

They caught one of the students using a batch of my poems
as a human shield. This student was so deluded by her
colonial education she actually thought that poetry
had the power to prevent rubber bullets from
penetrating her skin, that non-rhyming
poetry was a kind of muti that would
make her impregnable. The cops,
none of whom had ever finished
high school, whispered to her
while they were bending

over and cocking their
guns, they whispered
softly, "Don't go
changing, to
try and please me..."
the lyrics to an old Billy Joel
song but sung in the style of Barry
White and then they proved to the student
that poetry versus rubber bullets
is a poor way to measure
the state of the
nation

III

Once there was a time, you can still dimly remember it,
when you and your comrades used to laugh at all the
shitheads around you, blind and unseeing as they
were because of having their heads stuffed firmly
up the assholes of their leaders. Then, slowly,
gradually, in increments of infinitesimal mini
scularity, your own vision started to cloud
over until, how long ago was it? Recently,
fairly recently, or perhaps a lot longer,
time is very hard to tell when you're
in a colon; you noticed that all
you could notice now were
the occasional movem
ents of your leader's
bowels, as the
brown faecal
matter of his
leavings flowed
over your nose in
between the tiny little
breaths you dared to take.

It was interesting now because
the ostensible difference between
you and your leader was not only that
you were a shithead and he wasn't; but,
more significantly, he told his own lies where
as you repeated his lies verbatim. Perhaps some
distant memory of who you used to be inspired you
to make the herculanean effort of getting both shoulders
into your leader's rectum and yes, you did it, you actually moved
your entire body into the anal canal and crawled, wormlike to a
distant place where you could hear the hubbub and when you
got there, boy were you surprised; a million other shitheads
like yourself all in the process of turning to worms. You
were not alone at least, and now, in the comfort of
your leader's bowels you could all enjoy his con
stant feasting with only the occasional distur
bance of some fallen from grace shithead
being blown noisily out of your leader's
mighty asshole along with other dis
gusting faecal matter. Does it
never occur to you that it's
only a matter of time be
fore it's your turn to
be farted out?

IV

They turned the torture zone into a tourist site
the torturers all got jobs showing busloads
of foreign schoolkids where the tor
tures used to take place.
My waitress served
me a cheeseburger
with no sauce
She told me

that her
father
had
had his
fingernails
forcibly removed
in this very room

back in the day - that's
how she got the job, it was
her inheritance, she was a bene
ficiary of the new state's benevolence
And this party political broadcast was paid
for in denominations of twenty and fifty Fingernail notes
by the party concerned

V

We live in a country
where a white man's property
is worth more than a black man's life
We are collectively responsible for this atrocity
We have, collectively, the power to tear
the walls of this Prison down

We who are not dead yet.

Movement II

To him who has nothing it is forbidden not to relish filth.
To decompose is to live too, I know, I know,
don't torment me, but one sometime forgets.
The shadow in the end is no better than the substance.
                              Samuel Beckett

How I passed for white

My mother told me not to speak loudly in public
Not to speak loudly in private too, We don't do that
we're WHITE then she pinched the skin of my forearm
and when I yelped in pain she pinched me harder and she
held my burning pink skin up to the light and she said No matter
how little money we have no matter how hard our circumstance we've
always got one thing that they'll never be, WE'RE WHITE and the litany
of what we were and what they weren't went on and on you might say it all
came down to this We were all things good and they were THE DEVIL person
ified and it wasn't a joke and you couldn't laugh it off because the kind of white we
were was trash, no dear people, it wasn't as easy as that, for what i re
member most clearly about my sinister cousins was the occasional
hint in their tightly curled hair or the snubness of their noses that
the white that we supposedly were wasn't quite as clearly de
lineated as my mother would have preferred and maybe
that's why she moved us out of her family's orbit and
we left Joburg for Durban where she acquired an
English accent (from the movies I suppose)
and taught me to stick my little finger out
when drinking tea because That's how
we do it we're WHITE and so i was
trained in a million tiny tropes
that would serve not to give
me away and I'm 61 now
and it's taken me so
long to piece to
gether all the
stolen parts
because
despite
what

my
mother
taught me
i've never been
white i've always
been human and what
I'd like to say to my so-called
black humans is that all those so-
called whites who are running very
fast have been wound up very tightly
to run away from themselves. WHITENESS
is a theatre, a performance of exclusion, it only
means anything because of slavery which granted
those who performed the theatre an unspeakable power
of life and death over those excluded from the performance.
The echoes of that power to extinguish black life continue to re
sonate today in every sick incident that screams WHITE POWER
over the increasingly growing self-confidence and consciousness of
the black body. I cherish my so-called consciousness which rejects white
and black as simplistic illusions good for chess and pianos but not sophis
ticated enough to take on the human experience but nonetheless I un
derstand that I am embedded in a matrix of theatrical illusion that
murders some people without mercy, with impunity, merely be
cause they pass for BLACK.

Theophany

Eventually, after a lot of hullaballoo and noise
God appears on my porch through the flames.
I say 'God what pronouns do you use?'
God says' Hello Kaganof I don't do gender.'

I say 'God you think you the shit? I don't even do I.'
God says 'Watch out with that foul mouth of yours.'
I say 'God with all the fuckups you made you oughta be ashamed.'
God says 'I perfect.'

I say 'You perfectly mundane,
You created a world filled with sorrow and pain.'
God blushes and mumbles 'You got me there Kags.'
'And what about mortality, God? Why do we have to do die?'

God shrugs 'Ok good one, now please give me a break.'
But Kaganof's not in a break-giving mood.
'God why are there people still hungry
when there's so much left-over food?'
God says 'I gave you humans free will,
what you do with it is up to you.'

I say 'That's even more stupid than sacrificing your own son.
You could have made things decent,
With built-in permanent health insurance or better yet, no disease.
Instead you got all of us weeping and wailing on our knees.'

God says 'Kaganof if you so fucking smart
Why aren't you a millionaire yet, instead of
just another nagging customer with a list of complaints?'
I say 'God there's more to life than sheckels.'

God says 'Oh yeah tell me what?'

I say 'The very isness of your Being,
the possibility you exist, in a Quantum state
of is-God-here or is-God-isn't.
You fucked up in Auschwitz it's true,
you're fucking up in Gaza too,
but no matter how much evidence there is

that constantly piles up to confirm the *absence* of you,
we nonetheless keep on hoping and praying.'
God looks at God's Rolex and says 'Kaganof time's up!'
It's only then that I notice the Reaper

who's been hiding behind God, keeping schtumm
all through this fireside chat. The three of us pack up
my personal belongings which are not all that.
And off we journey to Heaven, which is,
as you probably already guessed,
just another neighbourhood in Hell.

Stellenbosched

Oh my word, the first drops of rain began to fall,
the violet cloud was torn by lightning,
there was a clap of thunder, and I, too,
was running down Helderberg into Dorp
as quickly as I could, heading for the station
to try and shelter from the approaching thunderstorm
all the wooden garbage covers had been ripped off
and around every one of these lidless rubbish points
a great circle of refuse strewn on the ground
as if it had erupted in a blast of subterranean filth
from a bank of dirt deep in the earth's core
and I was born a tiny woman and have been
growing smaller ever since this world, and
more particularly, Stellenbosch, has shrunk me
and the stench of it unbearable layer upon layer
of bad faith and false optimism bursting out
of the earth through the nodes of the wooden
refuse boxes that now emit gushes of liquid
shit brown gold has been struck in order
to fuel the motor of this septic lying place
to keep the living dead in place to feed
the newly mewling infants on in lieu of mother's
tit barren milkless hag tits hanging from me
and I lose a shoe as I start running to get away
from the foul stench of this filthy place
the air itself cancerous poison oozing
corruption into my lungs nothing fouler
than this place these streets and houses
ripped from their rightful owners ripped
grabbed taken the wounds paved over in
thick black tarmac of denial the bitter homeless
shoved into buckets and told to scrub themselves
clean of memory *dis kak* the *kak* stench billowing
in a great foetid cloud that will not disperse

jy mag nie so lewe jy hettie kaartjie ek onthou
en die kak brand that's the smell of shit on fire
it's long past the fan phase I was born myself
then I lost my shoe and running running to get
to the station before 8.30am but of course the 8.30
is cancelled *wat kan 'n mens anders maak?*
and it's waiting now til 9.08am when the next one
comes and everywhere around me as hard as a fist
the people stare with unblinking eyes there's no
memory left no whites in their eyes no compassion
only *vrek vrek* eyes *vrek jy god lewe ja is gevaarlik*
de helse vuur i can't hold it in anymore
the tiny me comes out in a stream a gout a gusher
nothing of me doesn't come out the past the future
even the seat of my pants and the shoe
that I swallowed but thought i had lost
all smelling of shit and it becomes apparent
that the inside of me is as much corrupted
and rotten as Stellenbosch itself
not a molecule undetected and or
unperverted then the train comes in
and I lead with *myn* elegant foot
the one that's become unshoed or is it I that's
become unhinged? And I step discretely
over the pile of me that I vomited up and
into the train carriage that speeds off
no windows it's freezing and the walls
all stickered over Dr. Zhaid penis
enlargement lost lover win lotto/casino
0736246111 Dr. Happy penis problems
all unfinished jobs 0742176931 and I'm
feeling sad
so I call Dr. Happy
and just then two blind singers
stand up
and start stumbling

down the length
of the carriage
singing awfully
out of tune
but with
great gusto *"the Holy Spirit will come down and everyone will be saved,*
everyone will be saved,
everyone will be..."

Palimpsestina 4.33

Here the reader begins
in abrasion
and line erosion,
as if the poet did not (completely)
                          trust words.

Cartloads of their bodies were
thrown into the sea.

and very close to a barbed wire fence.

The poem is about
our perception
again and again.

Nothing happens, there is no entertainment.

Palimpsestina 4.33a

Here the reader begins with the confrontation
and the landscape is *in* me.

Several cuts to closely-whispered words of the barbed wire
resulting in abrasion
and line erosion, the breaking up of stanzas

into smaller phrases.
as if the poet did not (completely) trust words.

Through the movement of the lines of text, the reader actively
pushes the image into the background,
asitisimpossible toconcentrateonimage
andtext atthesametime:

Cartloads of their bodies were transported every day
or thrown into the sea.

This
is not a still poem
but a moving poem,

You are left for a moment to linger and/or endure.

and very close to a barbed wire fence.

The poem is about
entertainment.

Palimpsestina 4.33 threatens to elude our perception
again and again.

Nothing happens, there is no entertainment.

Palimpsestina 4.33b

Here the reader begins with the confrontation
of image and sound, no further information is provided.

The envoi; this time a flat-toned ambient song sets in,
which exerts a meditative pull.

Nothing happens, there is no entertainment.

While the poem remains in its position,
it is never completely still, but is always
slightly in motion.

So it's about sound and landscape
and the landscape is *in* me.

Several cuts to closely-whispered words of the barbed wire
follow, focusing on its structure, the spikes,
their materiality—but also on the space it encloses.

So these word particles are moving by a series of low
tension impacts across the palimpsestic surface,
resulting in abrasion
and line erosion, the brea
                         king up of stanzas

into smaller phrases.

The words in *PS.4.33* are therefore not supplemented
by sound, but the story of the genocide
and its extraction infrastructure is also told
                        at the level of sound,
as if the poet did not (completely) trust words.

Sound is understood here as experience.

In doing so, *PS.4.33* undermines the hegemony of the word.

In *PS.4.33* the sound is present, it is not pushed
into the background; the sound
rather writes itself *into* the stanzas.

It features a group of malnourished
prisoners of war—men, women, children—a
figurative portrayal of the genocidal violence
that the poem seems to have explicitly avoided up to this point.

Through the movement of the lines of text, the reader actively
engages with the text and concentrates on the words,
which push the image into the background,
asitisimpossible toconcentrateonimage
andtext atthesametime:

> Cartloads of their bodies were transported every day
> over to the back beach, buried in a few inches of sand
> at low tide and as the tide came in, the bodies went out,
> food for the sharks.

The dead were also buried in individual graves
or thrown into the sea.

Wooden poles with barbed wire moving slightly in the wind
can be seen in the foreground,   birds fly overhead.

This and the slight movement of the palimpsestina itself
are a constant reminder that it is not a still poem
but a moving poem, in which the sun
begins to disappear below the horizon.

You are left for a moment to linger and/or endure.

Palimpsestina 4.33 sort of goes back to where it started,

the stanzas positioned in plain sight
and very close to a barbed wire fence.

The poem is about sound, about sound as an experience,
but also about contemplation.

Nothing happens, there is no entertainment.

Palimpsestina 4.33 focuses on the issue of perception,
attunement to the violent history of genocide
and what remains of it,
but also to what threatens
to elude our perception
again and again.

It is a dark poem
with the sun setting
in the background.

It is important that the reader
feels imprisoned
while reading this poem.

Nothing happens,
there is no
entertainment.

MOVEMENT III

The Palimpsestina

The Palimpsestina,
about which I will speak today,
          is constituted around
          an aesthetic
          and an ethic
                    of the fragment.

I

dust

from the unconscious

festered

due to the gradual deterioration
of language and

is also

operating in

that asymptotic border zone

to complete the relational loop

again.

This
is not a love song

II

The palimpsestina reveals densely packed dust
from the unconscious

      (perhaps

         she festered.)

We can now turn our attention to impersonal spillage

and a fragment
of *emergence,*
of *erasure,*

due to the gradual deterioration of the unconscious.

Colonised by vinegar-syndrome,

the palimpsestina is driven by the fear of language decay and
is also an aesthetic-ludic practice,

operating in both the bucket

of forgotten miners

holding on

to fragments

from the unconscious,

to complete the relational (Möbius) loop.

Begin again.

task
language
violence
meditation
abuse
mass transformities
polyphonic

III

incantation
erupts from the edge of language,
a love song actually moves,   not merely moving
gaps in ekphrasis and confession,
time unleashed from language as a means to an end
a way out of the machinic systems we claim to reject
schizophilic, ever-disintegrating
                      form
without saying we lack language
adequate to history we jiving.

>   gaps   in   narrative,
> a landscape of ekphrasis and confession,
> time unleashed from a dank, hiss
> (and history)
>   of relentless radio static

IV

language-machines
making possible
a certain concatenation of events
a paranoiac system
belonging solely to the symbolic order
of the palimpsestina

                The act of writing nevertheless finds
mistakes, blunders, ruptures, hiatuses, glitches, etc
threatening always to relegate language to
the impossibility of ending.

'This bucket of living death
overwhelms and nauseates
my throat and entrails,
while my heart invariably
shifts my thinking
to the fear of language'
      Nicola Deane
    and
     the palimpsestina works across consensus
reality
  and quantum time –

      a temporal depth, the paradox
      of bodies 'deserted by capitalism'.

V

The palimpsestina reveals

something

catastrophic

densely packed dust

from the unconscious

      (perhaps profoundly she festered.)
We can now turn our attention to
a fragment of found text more historically charged
than different images of *emergence*
of the traces of *erasure*,

known as *scriptio anterior* (former writing)
Colonised by the growing grime on the
                                crest of the koppie,
signalling a sporous
                                invasion, suffering from
vinegar-syndrome,
                                this bucket of living death
invariably shifts
                                my thinking to the fear of
police and is also
an aesthetic-ludic practice, driven by
impersonal spillage operating on the bucket

of forgotten miners in that asymptotic border
zone

of fragments for the future to behold and decode,

since the the palimpsestina   is driven by impersonal s p i l l a g e
from the unconscious, there   will always be forever lost parts,
but time is made visible   (historical) through the evidence
in the koppie to complete   the relational (Möbius) loop.

Begin again.

      black
      refrain cuts off
      raucously,
      and suddenly,
      They are laughing raucously

End of Part 1

VI

a crisis in language
epistemological paralysis
of infinite transitivity
the presence of what is absent
                            (that poem which is not yet)
is something dizzying
of ontological
      *im***possibility**

the voice shouting 'cease fire'
is the only real thing
remembering
and anticipating 'the world'

The palimpsestina is driven
by impersonal spillage
from the unconscious

VII

We hear in the background the sighing and groaning
of other voices - which gradually change
into moans and shrieks.

The koppie is hiding a violent gesture,
identity the bogus nothing more than
a Chat GPT nevermind
nevertheless yak yak yakkety yak in the vile bile
tick-tiktoking Insta identity,
sometimes interrupted by a dry cough,
zero point of which is all yada yada yada
groping around beneath more nevermind
traces of delulu sound mingle deliriously
everywhere rapidly accelerating post-
human stroboscopophiliamachinic
bilebloodburst behind the cutefaçade
decohere out of an irreducible
difference vortex, feedback,
signal   without receiver

Envoi
      advancing identities simply transform
      mind muscles into grid of
                      flesh and an autopsy.

Beckett tells us "nothing,

starts seeping through."

VIII

incantation
polyphonic
'cutting-room floor'
replication
erupts from the edge of language,
a love song to snippets of dialogue
actually moves, not merely moving

escape from language as a means to an end
a way out of the 'nothing, starts seeping through'
The palimpsestina forces us to reclaim part of
the machinic systems we pretend to reject.
a
schizophilic, ever-disintegrating narrative
created out of dispossession and estrangement

a form
without compromise
saying one thing:
                            we lack language adequate
                                                  to 'cease fire'

in that asymptotic border zone
between multiple levels of
feverish impulse
I was holding on
to the remains of a massive anarchival
process

IX

Here the reader begins
in abrasion
and line erosion,
as if the poet did not (completely) trust
                                          words.

Cartloads of their bodies were
thrown into the palimpsestina

and very close to a barbed wire fence.

This palimpsestina is always about
                                  our perception
                                  again and again

Nothing happens, there is no entertainment.

The events at the koppie threaten to elude our perception again and again. Nothing happens, there is no entertainment.

X

" The palimpsestina reveals itself again not (only) as erasure

Nothing ever disappears
completely, evidence of the
catastrophic:
        two glass bottles of densely packed dust

We can now turn our attention to preserving the small tin
containing a tightly bound cluster
of rusted staples and paperclips

and a fragment of found text is often more poetic

and more historically charged

than a phenomenological experience

of framing different images of *emergence*

such as the painting term *pentimento*

whereby previous marks or forms emerge

by the effects of the traces of *erasure*,

known as *scriptio anterior* (former writing),

due to the gradual deterioration of infinite layers of contents and contexts available when all perspectives invite their inevitable ruination,

the p a l i m p s e s t i n a is thus
driven by impersonal spillage
from the collective unconscious ('cease fire')

the project is driven towards the unmasking of smothered bodies.

It is also an aesthetic-ludic practice, ie. the palimpsestina
is driven by perpetual spillage from the container of
remains
to the forgotten bodies in traces
of that process of disintegration
present clues in the fragments
for the future to witness and decode,
since the palimpsestina is *a coding system*
          Begin again."
          Nicola Deane

    black bodies
    invisible black
    'No more laughter, prepare for tears.'
    But this is immediately followed by
    laughing.
    They are laughing raucously.

End of Part 2 Part 3 Follows

XI

particled language
absurdity
meaning
framed.

volatile
degeneration
of the source

a dust of events
uselessly complicated
koppie.

meaning is hysteria,
and stuck **together.**

a network of mirrors
obliterates the contours
of the original fire**line.**

The koppie forces us to become part

of the machinic system

we claim to reject.

XII

The time of the koppie is aways an ekphrasis and a confession,
time unleashed from chronology and prediction
time which resides in a dank, hiss (and history)
of relentless radio static escaping from language that merely *means*,
language as a means to an endling
a way out of the exhaustion of definition and concrete meanings,
an onslaught of scrolling text
the poem actually moves, not merely moving
       through the gaps   in   narrative,
only a landscape of koppie taal,
a text body whose shape   its meaning doesn't quite   fit
text created and then destroyed,   relegated to the 'cutting-room floor'
text-expanding replication
               erupts from the constant and so on, and so on
at the edge of language
transcend language
into a love song to liberation
not neutral
so fierce, so fraught
    snippets of dialogue
but we cannot understand it
    schizophilic, pataphysical ricochet of puns and word-play,
an ever-disin
  tegrating narrative
about the ever-disint
    egrating direction ('south')
created out of dispossession and estrangement.

        Voice-over: 'They are laughing raucously.'
        followed by fade out to an ostensible end.

XIII

Here the reader begins with the confrontation
    and the landscape is *in* me.

Several cuts to closely-whispered words of the barbed wire
    resulting in abrasion
    and line erosion, the breaking up of stanzas

        into smaller phrases.
        as if the poet did not (completely) trust words.

Through the movement of the lines of text, the reader actively
    pushes the image into the background,
    asitisimpossible toconcentrateonimage
    andtext atthesametime:

Cartloads of their bodies were transported every day
    or thrown into the wasteland.

You are left for a moment to linger and/or endure
    very close to a barbed wire fence.

        constant restatements or
        reappropriations or
        accumulations of
        perversities

XIV

How is one to read these miners' disappearances,
    this dimension of where things are *not* in the scene?

Any fragment bears each fragment's fragile mutilation,
    which is to say the very form of mutilation, in it.

This mathematical transitivity is founded on grammatical
    transitivity, and the mise-en-abîme of transitivities
    extends so long as the commanding officer's voice
    has not yet declared 'cease fire'
    to this expanded field of presences.

    The Palimpsestina is
    marked by forms of obsession,
    repetition and rumination, the explicit chain
    of names in the palimpsestina takes this broader logic
    and literalizes, or radicalizes, presence,
    a fitting anti-narrative for the palimpsestina's crumbling
    fragments about Marikana.

        Envoi

    The line, *They are laughing raucously*,
    repeated and slowed down,
    beyond which there is nothing.
    They are laughing raucously
    the unconscious
    functioning as a methodology
    They are laughing raucously

End of Part 3 Part 4 follows in a few minutes

XV

> The task is not only to change the world
> but also to find an adequate language
> with which to understand
> one's own participation in it.

ANDRIES NTSHENYEHO
killed by police.

Language that is an incantation
against the power structures
that continue to propel
our society toward violence.

ANELE MDIZENI
killed by police.

Language that allows for a meditation on the
theme of power: in politics, in the subjugation
and abuse of other cultures,
and in our divided selves.

BABALO MTSHAZI
killed by police.

Language that is astutely attuned
to the pressured, violent,
mass transformities forced upon us.

BONGANI MDZA
killed by police.

Language that evokes the polyphonic,
the democratic,
the multitude.

BONGANI NQONGOPHELE
killed by police.

Language that, by inviting
multiple interpretations,
invites the reader's participation
in the creation of multiple meanings.

BONGINKOSI YONA
killed by police.

In the palimpsestina each object, image, instant,
becomes hyper-loaded with language,
roiling inside a text body
whose shape it doesn't quite fit.

FEZILE SAPHENDU
killed by police.

In the palimpsestina, language becomes dismantled
and reassembled every instant by what it *isn't*
suggesting reams of text created
and then destroyed,
relegated to the "cutting-room floor."

JACKSON LEHUPA
killed by police.

This text-expanding replication goes so far out

that no matter what is in the palimpsestina,
there is always more beyond it,
giving definition to the space
of the as yet unseen self.

JANAVEKE RAPHAEL
killed by police.

Referred to by Deleuze as the "out-of-field,"
this space erupts from the constant awareness
that around the seen there is a larger set,
and around that a larger set, and so on, and so on.

KHANARE MONESA
killed by police.

Here the horror of unspeakable violence, and the joys
and challenges of reclaiming the body and sexuality
after violence, lie in what ends up *not* depicted
in the palimpsestina, what is always just there
at the edge of language, off-page.

MAFOLISI MABIYA
killed by police.

This "out-of-field" language always sets the tone,
a deep-seated feeling of regret or nostalgia or love
or hopelessness.

MAKHOSANDILE MKHONJWA
killed by police.

The poet's response to history is to transcend language,

to convert language into image,
          and image into music —
    and not just any music,
but a love song to liberation.

        MGCINENI NOKI
        killed by police.

Language is not a neutral tool,
  the history of the peoples who belong to a language
and the hegemonic forces that would suppress
  or obliterate both the language
     and their people
         are what make the palimpsestina so fierce, so fraught.

        MODISAOTSILE SAGALALA
        killed by police.

              The palimpsestina contains
                    snippets of dialogue,
        but we cannot understand it.

        MOLEFI NTSOELE
        killed by police.

  We are compelled to see
the individual names and letters,
    all the letters of the alphabet,
        perpetually and indefinitely.

              MONGEZELELI NTENETYA
              killed by police.

                    The narrative, when it does come,
                              is delivered in an onslaught
                                     of scrolling text.

                    MPHANGELI THUKUZA
                    killed by police.

              The textures of the lines and stanzas
                 start to take on a strange form,
         as when you stare at a word too long
                 and it begins to morph
                         into something unfamiliar.

                         MPHUMZENI NGXANDE
                         killed by police.

                              It is as if the palimpsestina
                                         actually moves,
                              is not merely moving.

                         MVUYISI PATO
                         killed by police.

          Everything comes to us
         through the holes,
                  in the seepage,
                         through the gaps in history.

                         MZUKISI SOMPETA
                         killed by police.

                              There is no narrative,
                                         only a landscape

of the massacre of language.

NKOSIYABO XALABILE
killed by police.

The time of the palimpsestina
is aways 15:53,
Thursday 16 August, 2012.

NTANDAZO NOKHAMBA
killed by police.

A dawn of singular intensity; both an ekphrasis
and a confession, a meditation and a mirror on time;
time unleashed from chronology and prediction;
time which resides in a dank, drunk, sordid hiss
(and history) of relentless radio static.

PHUMZILE SOKHANYILE
killed by police.

The palimpsestina's attempt to escape
from a language that merely *means*,
language as a means to an end,
language that stifles
as much as it could possibly liberate.

SEMI JOKANISI
killed by police.

The palimpsestina seeks a way out
of the exhaustion of definition

and concrete meanings
('cease fire').

STELEGA GADLELA
killed by police.

Beckett tells us 'To drill one hole
after another into language
until that which lurks behind,
be it something or nothing,
starts seeping though.'

TELANG MOHAI
killed by police.

The palimpsestina therefore exists
within a multiplicity
of positions,
modes,
and liberatory impulses,
modalities.

THABILE MPUMZA
killed by police.

The undecidability and multiple subject positions
in this palimpsestina are not postmodern strategies
of evasion but culturally specific modes of challenging
the relegation of private and public,
personal and political,
to separate spheres.

THABISO MOSEBETSANE
killed by police.

Here the muddying of the distinction
between freedom
and oppression, politics and sexuality,
victim and victimiser,
violator and the violated is methodological.
None of it meant to be.
Subconsciously. Inevitably.

THABISO THELEJANE
killed by police.

The palimpsestina forces us
to consider our own complicity;
to examine the ways in which we,
quietly and through inaction,
become part of the machinic systems
we claim to reject.

THEMBINKOSI GWELANI
killed by police.

At once strange and estranging, the palimpsestina
is a schizophilic, pataphysical ricochet of puns
and word-play, allusions and collusions,
superimposed into an ever-disintegrating narrative
about the ever-disintegrating direction
called *"South Africa."*
A namestate created out of
dispossession and alienation.

THOBISILE ZIBAMBELE
killed by police.

The poet
is no stranger
to estrangement.

JULIUS MANCOTYWA
killed by police.

The palimpsestina constitutes a lifelong search
for a form that might create the internal imaginative
condition for the refusal of oppressive state narratives,
and a determination to live, love, and speak
without compromise from the ground
of that refusal, no matter
how estranged or estranging the results.

JANEVEKE LIAU
killed by police.

If the palimpsestina is saying any one thing
it is that we lack a language adequate
to the history we are living.

HENRY PATO killed by police.

MICHAEL NGWEYI killed by police.

PATRICK AKHONA JIJASE killed by police.

CEBISILE YANA killed by police.

KHAWAMARE ELIAS MONESA killed by police.

JOHN LEDINGOANE killed by police.

THAPELO ERIC MABEBE killed by police.

TEMBELAKHE MATI killed by police.

SANDI TEYISE killed by police.

MLANDULI HENRY SABA killed by police.

        Then the word was made flesh
           Words like bullets shot
         Will it be your turn next,
          To be killed by police?

This
    is not a love song

XVI

If this palimpsestina is unrecognizable in its mode of address,
    if the semiotics of the death count
    become pure cadence and rhythm
    to which no response is possible
    or adequate (the truest sense of the monological),
    this is not a case of form obliterating sense,
    but of the sense of deferral functioning
    as the impossible assimilation of this massacre scene
    into the word 'democracy'.

As the meat of the decaying palimpsestina fades,
    we hear of the hillside post-mortem that it is
    all 'hair and skin and blood
    and flesh and them and them and them...'
    and suddenly,
    They are laughing raucously

The Palimpsestina, about which I have spoken today,
is constituted around an aesthetic
        and an ethic
of the fragment.

XVII

We are therefore ill-equipped to read
        the ephemeral traces, non-appearances,
        self-erasure and the violent disappearances
        that structure the destructured palimpsestina
                built on ruins, it is constituted
        around the koppie's devastation of origin or presence.

this bucket of living death overwhelms
and nauseates my throat and entrails,
while my heart invariably shifts my thinking
to the fear of language, since the palimpsestina is *a coding system*.

There will always be missing, dispersed, or forever lost parts,
for time is made legible through the evidence
of dust in the palimpsestina
but this is immediately followed by
laughing.

They are laughing raucously.
        repeated and slowed down,
beyond which there is nothing.

        Voice-over: 'cease fire'

Coda

At this point, the striking miners run down the hill
towards the officers
the koppie erupts into a performance
where dead miners are the score
for a broken music of bullets a *riotous deathscape*
a miner's body undermines all coherency
with the vermiculation of its bullet holes
And there is I think something intrinsically psychoanalytic
which brings The Palimpsestina into the fold of death
or rather into the fold of a kind of living along with death,
which we know as melancholia.   Melancholia
precisely as the resurgence of a loss here in front of us. A past
instant made insistently, incessantly, impossibly present. So
in the end, a long day went down, down the steep koppie,
down right down into, with closed eyes,
and I remember going to the basin
and washing my face seven times and opening my eyes
and still being blind
and felt incredibly
abused, I think,
and I realized there was, there was something here,
that cannot be believed or I cannot be believed.
That for me was the moment
of fundamental friction.
Saying to the koppie,
stop my eyes.
Stop my eyes.

MOVEMENT IV

While confabulation is pathological by definition, all people include an inventive (and thus spurious) element in their remembering. Indeed, it seems valid to say that all remembering depends heavily on reconstruction rather than on mere reproduction alone. Among those affected by amnesia, reconstruction is especially drastic, inventive, and error-prone, particularly in regard to chronological sequence. The difference, therefore, between ordinary and grossly amnesic confabulation may well be one of degree rather than kind.

https://www.britannica.com/science/memory-abnormality/Paramnesia-and-confabulation#ref386888

Stellenbosched Again

The train began to rumble over the bridge
and, tearing myself away from my battered
copy of *We Who Are Not Dead Yet*, I pressed
my face against the empty space where the
window should have been, cupping my
hands to blot out the bright carriage light
and though it was still only evening,
not even late evening, through the winter
landscape of garbage I could see a mass
of hundreds of individual fires burning
somewhere in the distance, pools of light
shimmering for little clusters of shivering
skarrelaars who made their living
in the massed garbage heaps that used to be
rolling countryside and the doors began to
slam at the end of the carriage as passengers
with suitcases on their heads started to make
for the exit, colliding with some orphaned
children and young girls coming in to sell
their bodies for protection, shaking dry
their wet hands because there was either
no towel in the lavatory or else it was too
wet and dirty to use the train was approaching
Stellenbosch outside you could make out
the lights of the station and, somewhere
beyond them, lines of broken street lights
disappearing into the distance, the glimmering
level-crossing hut, the dipped headlights
of cars waiting to cross the R44 and then
heaving slowly in sight directly below
the window, the high flood-lit platform

itself, blood splattered from all the black
escapees from previous windowless
Metrorail trains that hadn't quite made it
to the other side in time, and then the station
building with its brightly lit windows
that were almost all of them broken and
everywhere figures covered in vomit or
faeces or a combination of both, in the
restaurant, the waiting-room, at the ticket
office, by the newspaper kiosk and the train
finally stopped just beyond the station
building and once again the doors began
to bang and people milling around trying
not to step in the piles of garbage of vomit
of diarrhoea some running along in search
of their carriage others jumping coatless
out of the windowless window frames
on the look-out for beer or nik naks
three for five rand and it was extremely
easy in the foetid nauseous stench of
Stellenbosch station to imagine
that one had arrived in Hell.

When I arrived the next morning
at my office on 10 Marais Street
at precisely 8am my usual morning
starting time after leaving my modest
one bedroomed flat in the Serenahof
complex on the corner of Helderberg
where I had woken up bolt upright this
morning at 4.30... in the throes of a
nightmare, my skin was putrefying
and peeling off in layers of fatty

tissue with horrendous pores...
not even zombies look that bad
and, as one does in a dream and
momentarily uncertain about
whether I was awake or indeed
merely dreaming that I had woken
up but nonetheless needing or
dreaming to need the urge to defecate
and my blood pressure and cholestrol
being what it is I was taking no chances
and having rushed out of bed burst
into the toilet and onto the lavatory
seat cold to my bum cheeks where
what commenced to erupt out of my
fundament was of such protracted
violence and volume that when I fleetingly
looked down at the bowl it was not merely
filled but in fact thickly coated with the
leavings I might add here that the extent,
the surely excessive quantity of stool
made no sense to me I slowly climbed
the stairs up to my office number 2018
useless computer with no power looked
out of the window a beautiful day but all
of it useless without power and on my desk
opened to useless page 1 so why had I rushed
around Stellenbosch shaking with emotion
(I am not ashamed to admit it) with
the copy of *We Who Are Not Dead Yet*
in my hands? why in public on a train
had I avidly leafed through its flimsy
pages looking for places which I
seemed to have glimpsed before

and then why after seeing it bound
had I carefully placed the book which had
now become heavy on my desk like the
Bible keeping it there day and night?
why was I now on my way to Stellenbosch
yes not to Harvard or Oxford but precisely
to Stellenbosch? why was I reading this
Mwanaka book now, in a windowless
Metrorail carriage, beneath a wavering,
flickering electric light fitting, glaring
brightly at one moment, almost
extinguished the next according
to the speed of the train amid the slamming
of doors at either end of the carriage
by hawkers constantly coming through
and shouting nik naks nik naks four for
five rand four for five rand amid the
banging and slamming of all these doors,
with the rolling motion jogging my book
now to one side, now to the other,
and the smell of months and months and
possibly even years worth of uncollected
garbage wafting in through the windowless
panes which also let in the terrible cold
and let out the occasional suicide and
once or twice on the journey a hapless
murder victim who, having first been
weakened by multiple knife thrusts
then plundered for all valuables
and once thus fully extracted of all
that could be turned into cash was immediately
bleeding copiously great gouts of blood
defenestrated out into the vast mass

of garbage that once was this country's
countryside which somehow still lingered
although they had stopped running
all services long ago.

I am on a train again travelling by day
but it is winter time early August and to add
to it the train was heading north to Stellenbosch
so it was quickly darkening on the other side
of where the windows should have been
but this was Metrorail no windows bright
lights of Belville station flashing into view
and vanishing again behind me like the
gathering of some invisible harvest each
filth-veiled suburban platform with its
fleeting row of broken lamps melting
into one single ribbon of obsolescence
decay neglect and ruin the dull drone
of a station rushing past as if the train
were roaring into my traditional healing
the sound amplified by the lack of windows
and beyond the endless stench of uncollected
waste and the violent sway of the carriage
from side to side pitching and rolling and
outside once complete darkness had fallen
on Kuilsrivier nik naks three for five rand
and in the window along with me no
reflection because no working lights
in the carriage and all the seated
passengers anxious afraid to sleep
in case of knife attacks I took from
the suitcase in the rack above me a
book I had brought especially for

the journey to Stellenbosch and I
opened it at page 1 and instead of reading
the book by the time the train had passed
Melton Rose station I had inserted myself
into the diegesis of page 1 platform 1
Eersterivier this was going to be an "I"
poem but I badly needed to shit or needed
to shit badly which is much the same thing
if you're stuck on a windowless Metrorail
train with a thousand other safe abortion
pills on their way to or from the slaughterhouse
called "work" where they let you clock yourself
in and police yourself all day until you clock
yourself out at night and then the tv polices
you to sleep where the dreams you have of
being free are as flimsy and almost falling
apart as the Lynedoch station sign or the
book that my uncle gave me I had taken
it to a binder who trimmed the pages
so that they lay together evenly and
enclosed the whole thing in a strong
cover on which he pasted the book's
original title page before I changed
the book's name and indeed before
I changed my own name in as far as
any name could ever be called mine—
We Who Are Not Dead Yet—and then
the train pulled into Stellenbosch station
and I rushed to get to a toilet and I ran
to my office on Marais Street and locked
myself into the Ladies Toilet and so much
shit burst out of the hole in between my
two globular ass cheeks that I was forced

to think about that other asshole God
and what would she think about my
blassphemy but Nietzsche, thank God,
went mad or, more grammatically
incorrect but somehow closer to,
or at least approximating truth,
Nietzsche, thank mad, went God.

The Disappearance of the Actress (Cento for Two)

I

Even as a child I avoided multitudes,
I detested crowds, the accumulation of people,
the concentration of vileness and mindlessness and lies.
Will anyone doubt that I am aware how incomplete

and debatable these verses are? It is a very painful fact
in human experience that each of us must go over
the same old ground of mental struggle and development.
But it is not the end; it is the beginning. I thought

that if I could put it all down, that would be one way.
And next the thought came to me that to leave it all out
would be another, and truer, way. No matter what happened next,
I'd crossed over to the other place, and the question

wasn't who should I trust, but who should trust me?
A voice comes to one in the womb. Who is speaking thus?
A man without a mask is very rare. His eyes
grow accustomed to the darkness.

At the age of eighteen he was sent
to a military academy, where he received intensive training
in the use of weapons of mass destruction. They say weapons
tend to favour the powerful. We're brought up to hide

our true feelings and just put on a good face in these situations.
A man without a mask is indeed very rare. One even doubts
the possibility of such a man. Meanwhile, the actress
slipped into unconsciousness, and then finally just slipped away.

"It's pitch black in here!" a voice shouted, "Come and look!"
A voice comes to one in the tomb. Who is speaking thus?
The Actress suddenly remembered, without any forewarning,
herself standing at the top of the stairs. Could it have been love

that I saw? Is it true then, what they say – that we become stars
in the sky when we die? There is no sound. Her breathing
slowed while her pulse quickened and became irregular.
And I begin running. The blood must have already,

in its own silent way, seeped inside.
But I must tell you that what I have said is not true.
You are not dead. You have not gone mad.
And now I see her acting as something sublime.

The punishment begins. The streets are empty.
The walls quivered, still he did not hesitate.
Then the fence of the stage appeared out of the mist:
endless lines of wire strung between reinforced-concrete posts.

And yet here I still am, and resolved to trudge on.
"I'll follow you. Wait," she said, without taking his hand,
"maybe you should play after all," and she disappeared
through a little side-door directly beside the piano.

He hardly recognised himself. According to conspiracy theorists,
there is only one possible explanation, only one pattern
that makes sense. The tiny ball sped around, stopped,
and the croupier slid some counters towards him.

"But this can't be." I said, feeling quite distraught.
"Have I gotten as old as all that?"
At the station he found lieutenant Moloi, barechested,

sitting at his desk, covered with sweat.

It was time to switch the lights on or go home,
but he stayed where he was. Now he lay naked
on the marble, his arms flung out. Outside it was pouring rain;
all at once, the season had changed. In her room

the actress begins to pack, but in a little while
she goes to sit by the window
and look at the twinkling stars and foaming waves.
She knows she won't sleep and has all the time in the world

to finish packing her suitcase.
"What is this?" she asked.
The actress' eyes were instantly withdrawn;
and she sat silently meditating, in a fixed attitude,

for a few minutes.
To speak is to act; anything which one names
is already no longer quite the same; it has lost its innocence.
Not all crimes, however, are so easily resolved.

The reality that I had known no longer existed.
It is rather curious to see how one works things into a pattern,
into a silhouette marked out as if with a pair of compasses
or into a memory, so that one always feels one must say:

"Once upon a time ..."

II

I was spinning out again, unravelling. The only way to do this
is to be invisible. Kill or be killed that's the law of survival.
I'm getting the order of events mixed up. I swing around –
nothing but the back of the train, accelerating into the darkness.

The instant that the blade tore open her flesh, the bright disk
of the sun soared up and exploded behind my eyelids.
I open my eyes. The floor seems to be undulating beneath my feet.
Suddenly her eyes widen. I pull back my gaze, focus my camera

and she starts getting small, small, smaller – until I lose sight of her.
Now it only remains for me to light a cigarette and go home.
Only now am I remembering that people die.
Does that include me? As a matter of fact I don't want to die.

The actress got up, walked along with the noise of the wheels,
her movements leaning against the direction of the train;
something was still rumbling inside, but she was quite exhausted,
and her face relaxed into a smooth mask with vacant eyes.

Once back in my bedroom, I was afraid.
Death was everywhere.
Was it possible to fall in love
with the same woman

over and over again,
every single day?
"Now you know everything. I am at your disposal."
Then she straightened her back, lifted her chin

and walked quickly
through the double doors toward the stage.
There was only one way
to stop the young actress' diatribe.

"You're dead," I lied. "Don't play the innocent with me!
You know exactly what I mean!"
Every time I see the grave, I get that empty feeling
where something was, and isn't anymore,

and will never be again. To write without desiring to
and without intending to: what is it that hides here?
An actress knows when she's giving a good performance –
she doesn't need to be told, I thought.

It takes a little time to grasp more or less what happened.
In a few hours it would be dusk. When he had eaten
it would be time to rest, and to plan his escape from the stage.
The first thing he discerned when he regained consciousness

was a woman in white. "Silence!" he shouted out.
They were both gripped by the fearlessness of people
who have lost absolutely everything – such fearlessness
is difficult to attain, but once attained, it endures.

I looked out of the window again. Silent as a tomb.
There is unfortunately no point in speaking of escape.
A breakthrough in the police investigation came
only when analysis of mall surveillance tapes

revealed images of the candidate and another man
following the actress at a distance. It was no longer
raining and the wind had died down. When they reached

the station, the train was already standing there.

I came home on the last train. And yet here I still am,
and resolved to trudge on. Nobody knows what I've done.
Her face was pale. It no longer showed expression.
He didn't understand, then and there, what his spirit

was on the point of understanding. Cunning is necessary
to spread the truth. A hush had fallen over the room.
What is fate anyway? The strange policeman opened his folder.
He pulled out a piece of paper and consulted it.

"Have you lived here long?"
The sight of her: As if she were posing
for an invisible photographer,
she surpassed the calm of the sunset.

And I did not wish to interrupt that.
Here is the house. It is green and white. It has a red door.
She went to her room upstairs to pack, and the next morning
said good-bye and, alive, cheerful, left the stage – as she thought,

forever.

I do not mean to confuse you.
There is no doubt that we need more bread,
better homes, better schools, more time,
better air to breathe and land on which to live.

That goes without saying. There is great unrest.

"He doesn't love me anymore!" thought the actress
once she was alone, already regretting her decision.

"Does that make me a villain?"
The performance had ended, the audience streamed out;

the applause still echoed in the empty hall. But the idea
of the spectacle as something to be acted out
and absorbed still hung in the air long after the last spectator
had gone home to sleep. Just because it is too late

doesn't mean it was always too late.
"I could not fall asleep, and began writing," the actress said.
I drew the curtains in my room, writes the actress,
took several sleeping tablets, and woke up twenty-six hours later

in a state of extreme anxiety. Upon which she only laughed
and said *Yes*. The state of complete indifference,
in which I then find myself, said the actress,
is, through and through, a philosophical state.

I get through the night, the terrible despair, you know,
that appears in the walls when I scratch them with my fingers.
You see," said the actress, "my nails are all broken off."
In the days that follow the actress herself becomes drifted over

with new words, her hair slowly straightens,
she ceases to be what she was and is replaced,
gradually, by someone else. She assimilates.
"What do you want me to do?"

she whispers to the empty white man she says she despises.
Then she'll make a speech about how naughty she's been
and how much uproar she's been causing
and how many white men she's ruined. "You must come in,"

she says to me, "and take a tea," and she bends and undoes
the hook of the wooden gate.
"I knew you'd come back," she says.
"I knew it.

He awoke at seven the next morning. Crossing the lake,
the candidate and the actress looked down at their reflections
in the still, black water. In their bloodied hands
they carried Okapi knives with razor sharp blades.

They appear to have left within ten minutes of the last murder,
and no clues have been found to their method of escape.
And now nothing.
I did not comfort you.

Never have I comforted you.
Then the blood-red sun burst resoundingly in his head,
and he saw nothing more.
The day flowed on. It was a Thursday.

Thursday 16 August.
It was 3:53pm. Now she was naked.
The dream of being invisible ... I looked more closely.
It was wet. It was a tear. That is how she sees it.

That is how she understands it.
Then, a sudden creak behind me;
I spun round to see the door swing to on its hinges with a soft,
inexorable click.

III

My head aches with writing.
I close my eyes. I don't live. I don't exist.
I hope to die as painlessly as possible. That's all.

It gets harder all the time, the actress once said.
Harder, yet easier too. One gets used to things
getting harder; one ceases to be surprised

that what used to be as hard as hard can be grows harder yet.
She speaks. "That is enough. I don't want to talk anymore.
It is past nine. If you want to go – "

He rises, and he leans forward and kisses her thrice
in the formal manner he was taught as a child,
left right left, bows, leaves.

This is not the scene I dreamed of. Like much else nowadays
I leave it feeling stupid, like a man who lost his way long ago
but presses on along a road that may lead nowhere.

Everything has been said and resaid on the subject
of this inevitable and beneficial separation. In the end

they had to carry me to the infirmary and feed me
through plastic tubes. Recite the sacred words.

Meanwhile the rumours accumulate. I am being born again.
He notes her paleness. Sometimes he just looks at her.

You approach death with a clear mind.
Everything is connected in the end.

The odd thing is I found it beautiful, my death.
Everybody wants to own the end of the world.

A moment later the ambulance was on its way to the next call.
In a blue coffin decorated with white lace,

his hands folded and his eyes closed, lay the candidate.
Then a rather strange scene took place. The actress came out
with a pale little face, her eyes downcast, and took her bag.

"Will you be staying with us long?" the actress asked
the candidate. "My eyes aint any good anymore,"
the candidate said. "I cant see it." And that was all.

Then everything becomes calm.

I devoted the rest of the morning to preparing for what I hoped
would be the last stage of my journey. Another glass,
in which the alcohol is rapidly growing old, is shoved

across

the table. The bodies are totally unrecognisable with brutal
injuries like these, says the policeman, nauseated,
despite having seen a thing or two in his line of business.

She reached her hand across the table and rested it atop mine.
"Happy endings are all I can do," she whispered. "I wouldn't know
how to act anything else." Then he put on his mask.

The sun was now low beneath the horizon.
Darkness spread rapidly.
Darkness drops like a knife.

But Death is not the enemy.
Indifference is the enemy.

I'm packing. Yes, we two, the actress and I,
we are busy packing, really packing everything up,

leaving, clearing out, tearing things apart, pushing and shoving.
She shuts her eyes ... She walked away without looking back.

She died for love.
But I don't want to.

Most of the rest you already know.
As the sun set, I pushed my way
through the crowds
and out the gates,
walking up into the hills
from which I could see the stage and all its actors.

The disappearance of the actress remains a mystery.
To this day I have not visited her grave.

Mmap New African Poets Series

If you have enjoyed *We Who Are Not Dead Yet*, consider these other fine books in the **Mmap New African Poets Series** from *Mwanaka Media and Publishing*:

I Threw a Star in a Wine Glass by Fethi Sassi
Best New African Poets 2017 Anthology by Tendai R Mwanaka and Daniel Da Purificacao
Logbook Written by a Drifter by Tendai Rinos Mwanaka
Mad Bob Republic: Bloodlines, Bile and a Crying Child by Tendai Rinos Mwanaka
Zimbolicious Poetry Vol 1 by Tendai R Mwanaka and Edward Dzonze
Zimbolicious Poetry Vol 2 by Tendai R Mwanaka and Edward Dzonze
Zimbolicious: An Anthology of Zimbabwean Literature and Arts, Vol 3 by Tendai Mwanaka
Under The Steel Yoke by Jabulani Mzinyathi
Fly in a Beehive by Thato Tshukudu
Bounding for Light by Richard Mbuthia
Sentiments by Jackson Matimba
Best New African Poets 2018 Anthology by Tendai R Mwanaka and Nsah Mala
Words That Matter by Gerry Sikazwe
The Ungendered by Delia Watterson
Ghetto Symphony by Mandla Mavolwane
Sky for a Foreign Bird by Fethi Sassi
A Portrait of Defiance by Tendai Rinos Mwanaka
Zimbolicious: An Anthology of Zimbabwean Literature and Arts, Vol 4 by Tendai Mwanaka and Jabulani Mzinyathi

When Escape Becomes the only Lover by Tendai R Mwanaka
وِيَسَ مَرُ اللَّيْلُ فِي شِفَتَي... وَالْغَمَام by Fethi Sassi
A Letter to the President by Mbizo Chirasha
This is not a poem by Richard Inya
Pressed flowers by John Eppel
Righteous Indignation by Jabulani Mzinyathi:
Blooming Cactus by Mikateko Mbambo
Rhythm of Life by Olivia Ngozi Osouha
Travellers Gather Dust and Lust by Gabriel Awuah Mainoo
Chitungwiza Mushamukuru: An Anthology from Zimbabwe's Biggest Ghetto Town by Tendai Rinos Mwanaka
Zimbolicious: An Anthology of Zimbabwean Literature and Arts, Vol 5 by Tendai Mwanaka
Because Sadness is Beautiful? by Tanaka Chidora
Of Fresh Bloom and Smoke by Abigail George
Shades of Black by Edward Dzonze
Best New African Poets 2020 Anthology by Tendai Rinos Mwanaka, Lorna Telma Zita and Balddine Moussa
This Body is an Empty Vessel by Beaton Galafa
Between Places by Tendai Rinos Mwanaka
Best New African Poets 2021 Anthology by Tendai Rinos Mwanaka, Lorna Telma Zita and Balddine Moussa
Zimbolicious: An Anthology of Zimbabwean Literature and Arts, Vol 6 by Tendai Mwanaka and Chenjerai Mhondera
A Matter of Inclusion by Chad Norman
Keeping the Sun Secret by Mariel Awendit
◻ سِجِلٌّ مَخْتُوبٌ لِتَعَاءه by Tendai Rinos Mwanaka
Ghetto Blues by Tendai Rinos Mwanaka

Zimbolicious: An Anthology of Zimbabwean Literature and Arts, Vol 7 by Tendai Rinos Mwanaka and Tanaka Chidora
Best New African Poets 2022 Anthology by Tendai Rinos Mwanaka and Helder Simbad
Dark Lines of History by Sithembele Isaac Xhegwana
a sky is falling by Nica Cornell
Death of a Statue by Samuel Chuma
Along the way by Jabulani Mzinyathi
Strides of Hope by Tawanda Chigavazira
Young Galaxies by Abigail George
Coming of Age by Gift Sakirai
Mother's Kitchen and Other Places by Antreka. M. Tladi
Best New African Poets 2023 Anthology by Tendai Rinos Mwanaka, Helder Simbad and Gerald Mpesse
Zimbolicious Anthology Vol 8 by Tendai Rinos Mwanaka and Mathew T Chikono
Broken Maps by Riak Marial Riak
Formless by Raïs Neza Boneza
Of poets, gods, ghosts. Irritants and storytellers by Tendai Rinos Mwanaka
Ethiopian Aliens by Clersidia Nzorozwa
In The Inferno by Jabulani Mzinyathi
Who Told You To Be God by Mariel Awendit
Nobody Loves Me by Abigail
The Stories of Stories by Nkwazi Mhango
Nhorido by Siphosami Ndlovu and Tinashe Chikumbo
Best New African Poets 10th Anniversary: Selected English African Poets by Tendai Rinos Mwanaka
Best New African Poets 10th Anniversary: Interviews and Reviews of African Poets by Tendai Rinos Mwanaka

Best New African Poets 10th Anniversary: African Languages and Collaborations by Tendai Rinos Mwanaka
ANTOLOGIA DOS MELHORES "NOVOS" POETAS AFRICANOS 10° Aniversário: Poetas Africanos Da Língua Portuguesa Selecionados by Lorna Telma Zita and Tendai Rinos Mwanaka
ABRACADABRA, by Olivia Ngozi Osuoha
DES MEILLEURS "NOUVEAUX" POÈTES AFRICAINS 10ᵉ Anniversaire : Poètes africains d'expression française by Geraldin Mpesse and Tendai Rinos Mwanaka
Taurai Amai by Cosmas Tasvika Manhanhanha
Nhemeramutupo by Oscar Gwiriri
Ntombentle: Selected Poems by Sithembele Isaac Xhegwana
African Poetry Anthology: Chapbooks, Vol 1 by Tendai Rinos Mwanaka, Lorna Telma Zita and Helder Simbad
Juices Of The Forbidden Fruit by Tapuwa Tremor, Mapaike
Like The Starry Night Sky, by Obinna Chilekezi
The Stench by Jabulani Mzinyathi
African Languages Poetry Anthology Vol 1 by Tendai Rinos Mwanaka
The Tear of an Ophan Child by Mwanaka Fombe
Best New African Poets 2025 Anthology by Tendai Rinos Mwanaka, Lorna Zita and Mondo Arnold Kobi

www.ingramcontent.com/pod-product-compliance
Lightning Source LLC
Chambersburg PA
CBHW071008160426
43193CB00012B/1973